Dr. Kathleen Tresness completed her undergraduate degree from the University of Wisconsin-Madison, in 2004 and obtained her PhD from the University of Minnesota in 2012. Dr. Tresness has worked in both private practice and mental health clinic settings for the past 10 years and is licensed as a psychologist in the states of Illinois and Minnesota. She currently provides psychotherapy and psychological testing to patients of many ages and she is owner of her private practice, Wild Meadows Counseling. She resides with her husband and two young daughters.

To my daughters, Elise and Hayley, who are responsible for my own embarkment into this wonderful journey of motherhood. I am so grateful to be your mother.

Dr. Kathleen Tresness

THE RESILIENT NEW MOM

9 Practices for Emotional Health

AUSTIN MACAULEY PUBLISHERS™

LONDON • CAMBRIDGE • NEW YORK • SHARJAH

Ordering Information
Quantity sales: Special discounts are available on quantity purchases by corporations, associations, and others. For details, contact the publisher at the address below.

Publisher's Cataloging-in-Publication data
Tresness, Dr. Kathleen
The Resilient New Mom

ISBN 9781649791344 (Paperback)
ISBN 9781649791351 (ePub e-book)

Library of Congress Control Number: 2023910880

www.austinmacauley.com/us

First Published 2023
Austin Macauley Publishers LLC
40 Wall Street, 33rd Floor, Suite 3302
New York, NY 10005
USA

mail-usa@austinmacauley.com
+1 (646) 5125767

I have had so many incredible people in my life that have not only helped me with this book, but have also helped me with my own motherhood journey. To my mother and father, for always supporting and encouraging me, throughout my life. Your unconditional love and support have guided me and have given me the strength and courage to live life to the fullest. To my husband, Jesse, and friends and family, who are part of my "village" and support system. I am forever grateful for the help you have given me throughout the years. To my teachers and coworkers who I have learned from and continue to learn from every day as a psychologist.

And last, but not least, to the moms out there who have inspired me and shown me the very definition of resilience. This book is for you.

Table of Contents

Introduction

It is within the journey of motherhood that a woman discovers how strong she really is.
– Anonymous

And so, the journey begins. And what a journey it will be! Motherhood is one of the most amazing experiences in a woman's life. With it often brings a wide range of emotions, including excitement, exhaustion, fear, but most importantly, happiness. While motherhood can be one of the most challenging journeys in life, it also brings great joy and rewards with it. It allows us to experience a love we've never experienced before. It helps us learn amazing amounts of patience and understanding. It shows us how strong we really can be.

The Incomplete Life Course

While it will be one of the most wonderful things a woman can do in her lifetime, becoming a mother can also be one of the biggest transitions she will face. Since motherhood is such an important job, one would assume that society would prepare new moms for this transition. Unfortunately, this isn't always the case. Because of this, many new moms may struggle emotionally and can have a difficult time adjusting to the changes.

If you are reading this book, I'm betting you are either preparing for your baby's upcoming birth, or you have just welcomed a baby not too long ago. As with any journey in life, you try to prepare yourself as much as you can for what lies ahead. To help prepare yourself for this journey of motherhood, you likely have read books about pregnancy or adoption, the birthing process, and how to take care of your newborn. You might read books that focus primarily on the baby and how to raise a well-adjusted child. And all of these things are, of course, important and helpful to learn. After all, you need to know what to do with that little one once he or she arrives! But while all of these are important things to learn during this journey, I believe that it is equally important to learn ways to take care of yourself emotionally through this process.

In addition to books, there are many classes new moms can take before or after the baby arrives. However, the vast majority of these classes focus on the birthing process or how to take care of the baby. Very rarely do I hear about classes that focus on the mother's emotional health and ways to guide them through the transition into motherhood. That's where this book come in. The purpose of this book is to equip new mothers, like you, with tips and strategies to help you feel emotionally strong and healthy during this transition.

So Why Is This Important?

It is important for new mothers to learn ways to more easily transition into motherhood because the transition can feel difficult at times. According to the Pregnancy and Postpartum Support website, it is estimated that up to 80% of mothers experience postpartum 'baby blues' or postpartum blues, while 15–20% of mothers experience more significant symptoms of depression or anxiety. Research shows that the marital relationship can also be affected. Following the birth of the first baby, many wives report decreased marital satisfaction (Gottman and Silver, 2007). There is no doubt that the transition into motherhood can sometimes be tough! As a new mom, not only are you facing many changes but you're likely also sleep deprived and exhausted. In addition, you have a new responsibility of keeping a tiny human alive! Talk about stress! And, you might feel like you don't know what you're doing half of the time with your new baby, and that self-doubt can add to that already existing stress. You might feel like you don't have the time to focus on other important relationships in your life, including the relationship with your partner. These things can all take its toll on any new mom. However, while motherhood can sometimes feel tough, I truly believe that there are things that new moms can do to make it feel just a little *less* tough. There are tools and strategies that can help new mothers better navigate the transition by making it a little easier.

Experience

As a psychologist, I have worked with many new mothers while they navigated their new journey into motherhood. It was apparent that many of these new mothers were struggling with similar issues and saying similar things. For example, they oftentimes struggled with their expectations about motherhood. They often talked about having difficulty connecting with their partners. Many times, they struggled with a loss of their old identity. I noticed they were so focused on the baby that they oftentimes forgot to take care of themselves. I noticed they were trying to do everything on their own because that's what they thought they were supposed to do. In addition, many of these new moms felt overwhelmed and struggled with organizing and prioritizing since the transition into motherhood began.

Having a baby can be one of the most rewarding and exciting times in a new mother's life...and...it can also bring on a new set of challenges to maneuver through. When a baby is born, it is common for the focus to be on the child. The problem, however, is that the mother may not get the focus and attention that she deserves throughout the transition. Through my experience, I have worked with many new mothers who are trying to navigate this new transition and find ways to better balance themselves. New moms may have difficulty balancing their multiple roles in the home and at work or difficulty attending to their relationship with their partner. They may also have difficulty with finding time to take care of themselves and in maintaining a sense of personal identity after the baby arrives. All of these things can affect the transition into motherhood.

Amy was a prime example of just how difficult the adjustment into motherhood could be. When Amy walked in for her counseling intake, it had been around three months since she gave birth. As we discussed in more detail about what brought her in for therapy, she began talking about all the changes she has been experiencing since her baby arrived. She talked about how her relationship with her husband feels different and they seem more emotionally distant from one another. She discussed how she loves her son, yet, she has had a hard time really bonding with him. She mentioned she is excited about her new role as a mom, yet exhausted, depleted, and run down. She was feeling overwhelmed with all the day to day responsibilities of the home: the laundry was piling up, her house was a mess, and she was eating chips and salsa for dinner because she hadn't made it to the grocery store.

Over the course of the next few sessions, we began to tackle these problems one by one. We talked about strategies to communicate more effectively with her husband and find ways to emotionally connect with one another. We explored ways she can bond with her baby to help foster that relationship. We discussed ideas to recharge her battery from being depleted through using self-care strategies. We talked about ways she can hold onto old parts of her personal identity. And we brainstormed how she can take back order in her home by exploring specific strategies that would help her feel more organized and less overwhelmed.

Amy's struggles can be common challenges that new moms often face as they are transitioning into motherhood. And the good news is, many of the difficulties new mothers face can be changed, and/or improved. And again, this is the goal of this book: to help new mothers learn ways to more easily navigate the transition into motherhood.

How This Book Will Help

The purpose of the book is to teach new moms, like yourself, tools and strategies that focus on emotional health, that will aid in your transition into motherhood. This book does this by exploring nine practices. Specifically, this book will help you reevaluate your expectations and beliefs about motherhood. It will explore ways to secure help and support from others and learn ways to bond with your baby. It will also help you identify and change problematic self-talk that can create self-doubt and negatively affect your self-esteem. This book will help explore self-care strategies to help create balance and examine ways to retain a sense of personal identity. In addition, it will address ways to evolve the relationship with your spouse or partner. This book will help you take back order into your life by discussing specific skills and strategies to incorporate into your daily routine. In addition to exploring the nine practices in detail, this book will also include a chapter on common roadblocks or obstacles that oftentimes get in the way of these practices being implemented. Ways to move past these obstacles are also explored further. While this book is designed to help new mothers adjust to motherhood, this is not a book designed to treat specific mental health issues, such as postpartum or perinatal depression or anxiety. If you are struggling with a mental health issue, it is important to seek treatment from a professional. There are many providers that specialize in these areas specifically.

One thing I hear over and over as a psychologist is *I know I'm supposed to take care of myself, but I don't know how*! Or *I know I should communicate better with my partner, but I just don't quite know how to talk in an effective way!* A lot of people *know* what they should do, but they struggle with the specifics about *how* to change or where to start. For these reasons, I wanted this book to include specific tools, tips, and strategies. While it is helpful to be aware of things that need to be changed, it is equally important to take action steps toward that change. Now, without further ado, a brief overview of the nine practices.

Chapter 1
The Nine Practices

Having kids – the responsibility of rearing good, kind,
ethical, responsible human beings – is the biggest job
anyone can embark on.
– Maria Shriver

A good friend of mine, Kelly, was thrilled to be a new mom. She had difficulty getting pregnant and after years of trying she finally was able to conceive and give birth to a beautiful baby girl. Kelly seemed to really love this new phase in her life. Yes, she was tired like many new mothers. Sure, she had her bad days. But overall, she adapted quite well to the transition into motherhood. Kelly seemed to have realistic expectations of herself and motherhood. She didn't strive for perfection, but rather strived to do her best. She had good self-awareness of her limits and when she needed help from others. She would tell me about her cute little routines she would do with her baby each day that really helped build their bond. Even on those bad days when it seemed things just weren't going right, she would find a way to get through somehow. Kelly seemed to utilize many of the nine practices that are covered in this book. So, what are the nine practices?

R: Reevaluate expectations and beliefs about motherhood

E: Establish a bond with your baby

S: Secure help and support from others

I: Identify and change problematic self-talk

L: Learn to incorporate self-care strategies

I: Incorporate all parts of your identity

E: Evolve the relationship with your partner

N: Navigate through SOS Mommy Moments

T: Take back order

While the rest of this chapter gives a brief overview of each of these practices, each subsequent chapter will explore each of these practices in more detail. But below is a quick introduction to these nine practices.

Practice #1: Reevaluate Expectations and Beliefs about Motherhood

We all have an idea about what motherhood will be like. Our expectations are oftentimes created way before our baby comes. As a new mom, you may have unrealistic expectations and beliefs about motherhood. You may think you can do it all on your own. You might think there is only one good way to do something. You might have the expectation that you should feel bonded to your baby right from the beginning. You might think that good moms aren't supposed to have bad days. You might think that good moms are supposed to know what to do, and that it should come naturally. You might compare yourself to other moms and feel that you are lacking or inferior because you don't think you have it quite as together as they do.

We oftentimes set ourselves up for failure by frequently setting unrealistic expectations that are unattainable. Later in the book, common problem beliefs that new mothers have are explored as well as strategies to change those unrealistic expectations and beliefs.

Practice #2: Establish a Bond with Your Baby

A lot of new mothers have a belief that they should instantaneously be bonded to their baby, as soon as he or she is born. In all actuality however, many new mothers struggle with establishing a close bond with her baby right away. Because of this struggle, they may begin to doubt their ability as a mother and their decision to become a mother in the first place. I've heard many moms talk about how they are just 'waiting' for that bond to happen. And yes, while that bond can gradually develop over time, there are also things you can do to help facilitate that bond. Dr. Meredith Small, a Cornell University anthropologist, says that "Bonding is not instantaneous, but a process – a relationship that grows from being together over time." Why is bonding with your baby important? According to research by Poobalan and colleagues (2007), there is a relationship between difficulty bonding and postpartum depression in mothers. Not only is bonding good for the mother but it is also important for the baby's development. Ways to evolve that bond between mother and baby are discussed in more detail.

Practice #3: Secure Help and Support from Others

One thing I have learned over the years in my role as a psychologist, is that we all need help sometimes. Whether you are a single mom or you have a partner in this journey, we all need help. There is a reason why it 'takes a village' to raise a child. Being a new mom can feel isolating and lonely at times. If there is one mistake that I see over and over again with the new mothers I work with, is that they try to do everything on their own, without help. Whether it's because they are afraid or embarrassed to ask for help, or they have an expectation that they should do things on their own, many new moms don't ask for help when they need it. All new moms need a support system to help navigate through this journey. Later in the book, we will explore in more detail ways to expand your village and recognize and ask for help when needed.

Practice #4: Identify and Change Problematic Self-Talk

Many people struggle with problematic self-talk, and new mothers are no exception. What is self-talk? Our self-talk includes the messages we tell ourselves. This could include the things we say out loud to ourselves or thoughts that we may have about yourself, what we are doing, and how we are feeling. For example, we might think to ourselves, oh man, I really stink at this parenting thing. That would be an example of a negative thought or problematic self-talk. Most of the time, we are not even aware of our thoughts and the judgments we put on ourselves. The issue with using problematic self-talk, is that it can affect our emotions and behaviors in a very negative way. Later in the book, we will explore common problematic self-talk examples as well as tools and strategies to challenge problematic self-talk.

Practice #5: Learn to Incorporate Self-Care Strategies

When talking about the importance of self-care, a good analogy is the battery metaphor. We are like a rechargeable battery in that our energy is constantly being depleted from all of the things we have to do in a given day. In order for us to 'work' properly, however, we need to recharge ourselves so that we can regain the energy needed to tackle our daily responsibilities.

For many new moms, their 'battery' is depleted, and they do not do enough recharging. As mothers, we give, give, give, and do, do, do. We are completely drained by the end of the day. It's exhausting! Many new moms fall into the trap where their battery is drained and they haven't figured out ways to recharge it. And when that happens, we feel tired, overwhelmed, and irritable. Essentially, our energy is low, both physically and emotionally. It is important for us to 'recharge' our battery through self-care strategies. In order to give, we need to have some energy in us to give in the first place. Common self-care strategies are explored in the Practice #5 chapter.

Practice #6: Incorporate All Parts of Your Identity

New mothers may struggle with the transition into motherhood for many reasons, but one of those reasons can be related to a feeling of loss in themselves as an individual. In other words, they feel their personal identity has changed. Their sense of self has changed. A very new and major role now is that of being a mother. While this is an extremely important role, it is important to remember that it is not our only role in life. Many times, in order for us to be good moms, we need to focus on all parts of our identity and the roles that make us who we are. It is important to focus on including parts of your 'old' self into your new experience. For example, new moms should continue to find time to engage in hobbies or activities that they love to do. There is this faulty belief out there that mothers are supposed to drop everything when they become a mom and solely focus on their child. However, for many new mothers, this strategy doesn't work and they are actually much better mothers when their other roles can continue to be included.

Practice #7: Evolve the Relationship with Your Partner

After a baby is born, the relationship with your partner can begin to change. Many times, it's for the better. It is an incredible feeling when you and your partner work together toward this important goal of raising a child. Many couples get through that first year of parenthood with their relationship even stronger than it was before. However, sometimes the relationship changes in other ways that create a challenge for the couple. Because of your new roles and responsibilities, you most likely will not have the same amount of time as you had before to spend with one another. You might forget to focus on your relationship with your partner because you are so focused on your baby. This chapter includes a discussion of common struggles that couples face in the relationship, post baby. Strategies to evolve and repair the relationship are discussed further.

Practice #8: Navigating Through SOS Mommy Moments

All mothers have had *those* days. You know, the days where it feels like nothing is going right. Those moments when you feel like you're drowning in the sea of parenthood and you desperately need to come up for air. Those moments where you're looking for a life vest, but you just can't seem to find one. I call those times SOS Mommy Moments. These are the moments when you feel you might lose your mind! It is important for every new mom to have tools to grab onto when in an SOS situation. Learning strategies to help you navigate through SOS Mommy Moments are crucial.

Practice #9: Take Back Order

During times of transition, we may notice our lives becoming disorganized and out of whack. In fact, I've heard so many new mothers say that one of the first things they abandon is order. It's hard to stay organized, especially when we don't feel we have the time or the energy! However, order helps us feel organized (both mentally and physically) and it gives us clarity. So, when we lose our order, we can feel anxious, overwhelmed, and exhausted. Therefore, we need to find ways to stay organized, both mentally and physically. Specific strategies are discussed later in the book to help us moms take back our order.

Afterword: Moving Forward and Getting Through Roadblocks

These practices discussed briefly above are geared to try to assist you in your journey of early motherhood. While it can be important to learn these practices and specific skills, it's even more important to apply them. What good are the skills if you struggle with applying them, right? The last chapter of the book focuses on ways to get through roadblocks or obstacles. Common roadblocks that may get in the way of implementing these practices are discussed, as well as ways to move through the obstacles.

Chapter 2

Practice #1: Reevaluate Expectations and Beliefs About Motherhood

There's no way to be a perfect mother and
a million ways to be a good one.
 – Jill Churchill

We all have expectations about what parenthood will be like. Some good, some bad. Some attainable, some not. Many of our expectations are based on what we have learned in the past. These expectations can be helpful in that they give us some idea of what may happen. When something is new or unknown, this can come in handy because we tend to like the idea of knowing what could happen next. It relieves our anxiety or fears about the unknown. Our expectations can be problematic, however, when they are unrealistic or too perfectionistic. They become a problem when they cannot be realistically met because they are unattainable or we have set our standards too high. Usually when this happens, we might feel that we have failed. We believe we are not good at what we are supposed to be doing. We get down on ourselves or feel disappointed. Unrealistic or perfectionistic expectations set us up for failure because they are impossible to achieve. They can oftentimes lead to disappointment when our experiences deviate from how we imagine they will be. I often see two common types of unrealistic expectations: expectations we place on ourselves as a parent, and expectations we have about how parenthood *will* be or how it is *supposed* to be.

Origins of Our Parenting Expectations

For starters, how do we develop our expectations about something? Specifically, our expectations about motherhood? Many times, our expectations originate from our own parents. We have seen behaviors and beliefs modeled to us. Or maybe we get our expectations from our close friends or family members who have recently entered parenthood. Just as often, our expectations come from media sources. We see things on TV, in movies, and social media like Instagram and Facebook. Media definitely has its perks, but it can be awful for setting unrealistic expectations about things. I have worked with many mothers who compare themselves to others on social media and begin to feel that they are less than, not good enough, and inadequate compared to what they see. Many new mothers struggle with feeling like they are lacking or inferior because they see other mothers on social media who appear to have it 'all together.' Yet what they forget or do not realize, is that what is shown on social media may not be an accurate representation of reality.

Identify Unrealistic Expectations

What is forgotten in those moments when we are staring at the perfect social media picture post, is that this may not be a realistic expectation of what typical motherhood is like. What is more realistic, is that while some days you might feel like you have it 'all together,' many days you will not. Motherhood is far from perfect. What is a more realistic expectation, is that there will be a variety of good days and bad days. That is normal. That is typical. This is a more realistic expectation. A good example of unrealistic expectations in motherhood comes from a former patient of mine, Jamie. She was a first-time mother who was really struggling with all of the demands of motherhood. She struggled with the endless list of responsibilities she had each day. She would openly talk about these challenges and how motherhood was not what she expected or thought it was going to be. As our sessions progressed, we began to really explore her expectations about motherhood and what it means to be a 'good' mom.

After looking into these expectations further, it was becoming more apparent that many of Jamie's expectations were unrealistic. For example, she believed that good moms were supposed to juggle all the responsibilities of motherhood with ease. That good moms were able to do everything on their own, without help. That if your child misbehaves, it was a reflection of bad parenting. Jamie put a lot of pressure on herself to be a 'perfect' mom. She often felt like she was 'doing it wrong.' She felt like a failure and felt like she was letting her husband down, her child down, and herself down.

Jamie had many unrealistic expectations for herself that were making her feel discouraged, overwhelmed, and frustrated. She was striving for perfection, yet this was not possible. As our sessions went on, however, Jamie began to realize that she was setting herself up for failure with her perfectionistic expectations. Jamie began to understand that many of her beliefs about motherhood and parenting were unrealistic and unattainable. That helped her begin to challenge her unrealistic expectations.

Another typical expectation I commonly hear new mothers talk about is that they believe they shouldn't need to ask for help and that it's a sign of weakness to let others help you. Or they believe they should feel bonded to their baby right from the start. Or that 'good' mothers are supposed to know what to do and it comes naturally to them. Think about this though: when you are learning anything new for the first time, you realize that there is a learning curve, that it takes time to figure things out, that you will make mistakes. Why would motherhood be any different? A realistic expectation is that you give yourself some compassion and understanding that you are not supposed to know how to do everything but you will learn along the way. What matters most, whether it's a new job or learning a new activity, is that you have the desire and are willing to learn and grow. A more realistic expectation is that you will make little mistakes, but you will likely learn and grow from them. Here are some common unrealistic expectations or beliefs I often hear about motherhood:

a) I should be able to take care of my baby without help.
b) I should recover quickly from childbirth.
c) If I struggle, I must be a bad mom.
d) If my baby struggles, I must be doing something wrong.
e) Asking for help is a sign of weakness.
f) I need to do everything perfectly to be a good mom.

Challenge Unrealistic Expectations

A good place to start is to ponder your own expectations about motherhood and question whether your expectations are realistic or achievable. Do you believe any of the expectations listed above? Do you have any others that should probably be challenged? To help identify whether an expectation is realistic or not, it can be useful to ask yourself:

- Is this expectation really working for me?
- How is this expectation affecting me? My family? My baby?
- Is there another way to approach this scenario?
- Is this helping me reach my goal?
- Does this help me get what I want or need?
- What are the pros and cons?
- What would I say to a friend in this situation?

After taking some time to explore your own expectations about parenthood, then you can challenge and replace the unrealistic expectations. For example, with the belief: *I should be able to take care of by baby without help*. A more realistic expectation would be to remind yourself that we all need help sometimes. In fact, in many cultures it is the norm for family members and friends to take turns helping out mom and baby during the first weeks and months of motherhood. Another example relates to the idea that if a mother or her baby struggles, that must be related to poor parenting. A more realistic expectation would be that it's perfectly normal to struggle at times. Both you and baby are adjusting to something new, and learning is part of that process. If you believe you need to do everything perfectly to be a good mom, then you will definitely set yourself up for failure because perfection doesn't exist. As I said, a realistic expectation is that we all make little mistakes and don't make the best choices as parents 100% of the time. Part of all journeys is to learn and grow as people. Motherhood is no different. We will all have moments where we may do and say things that are not 'perfect' and we realize we should have done something differently. What matters most is that you view these experiences as a learning experience. Just like most things in life, we need to learn and practice being a good parent. When you think back to when you started a new job, or even learned how to ride a bike for the first time, you made mistakes, but you figured it out. In motherhood, we won't do everything perfectly but it is important to have a willingness to grow and learn in the journey.

Release Expectations That Are Unattainable

As discussed before, some unrealistic expectations include the ones we place on ourselves. But others are expectations we have about how we think parenthood will go or is supposed to go. Sometimes we need to learn to let go of our expectations that, for whatever reason are just unattainable, and become more flexible with what we believe parenthood will be like. I learned the need to be flexible with my expectations right from the beginning of my parenthood journey. When I was pregnant with my first daughter, I went into my physician's clinic for my regular 34-week check-up. The doctor told me I had severe preeclampsia and I needed to go directly to the hospital. On my way to the hospital, I remember thinking, What? How can this be? I still have 6 weeks to prepare! I'm not ready physically or mentally for this! This is NOT what I planned or how I thought it was going to be! My baby shower was supposed to take place the following day. I was supposed to celebrate the upcoming arrival of my baby, eat good cake, open some presents. Now I was on the way to the hospital about to give birth. I was scared and felt unprepared. Less than 24 hours later, I gave birth to my baby girl. Because of her prematurity, she was moved to the NICU where she lived for 25 days.

This is how I started out motherhood for the first time. Obviously, this did not fit my expectations about what motherhood would be like. I had to grieve the loss of my expectations of what the first month of motherhood would be like. But this experience taught me an early lesson: that sometimes we need to be flexible with our expectations. We can feel sad, disappointed, or angry, when our expectations are not met or attained, but we also need to recognize the necessity of grieving and/or letting go of expectations that won't be met. I had to grieve and accept the fact that my daughter would be in the NICU for 25 days. I had to accept that I wouldn't be able to go to her and hold her in the middle of the night when she cried. I had to accept that a nurse would be doing those things that I felt like I should be doing as her mother. I grieved that loss and accepted that our story would be a little different than what is typical, but I can't control that. Acceptance of situations that are sometimes out of our control is oftentimes needed to move forward. Learning to let go and adjust when needed is one of the best tools you can learn as a new parent. In fact, you will have many times to practice this in the future!

Chapter 3

Practice #2: Establish a Bond with Your Baby

*There really are places in the heart you don't
even know exist until you love a child.*
– Anne Lamott

The bond that develops between a mother and her child is truly incomparable. However, it is a common myth that all mothers are instantaneously bonded to their baby, right from the start. For many new mothers, the bond they establish with their baby is one that gradually develops over time. I have worked with many new mothers who begin to doubt their ability to be a good mother and their decision to become a mother because they have struggled in bonding with their baby. Many new mothers who struggle with this are just 'waiting' for that bond to happen. That just one day, poof and the bond will be there. The problem is, this is not true for all mothers. Many times, the bond is gradually developed over time and not something that just happens out of the blue one day. However, I don't believe that this needs to be a passive process. I am a strong believer that there are many things one can do to help facilitate that bond.

As discussed early in the book, there is a correlation between difficulty bonding and postpartum depression in mothers (Poobalan et al., 2007). Not only is bonding good for the mother but research shows that it is also important for the baby's development. So, what can be done to actively work on your bond?

Increase Oxytocin

Likely, you have heard of oxytocin before. Oxytocin is a natural hormone in our bodies. It plays an important role during labor and post labor. It is the hormone responsible for bonding, attachment, and social interaction. People often refer to it as the 'love' hormone or the 'cuddle' hormone. Studies have found that oxytocin is correlated with levels of maternal-fetal bonding (Levine et al, 2007). One of the easiest ways to increase oxytocin, is through physical touch. When I was in the NICU with my daughter following her birth, I was introduced to 'kangaroo care.' Kangaroo care is essentially a method of holding your baby that facilitates skin-to-skin contact between the mother and infant. The infant is naked (except for a diaper) and the parent holds the infant in an upright position against their bare chest, usually with a blanket over the baby's back and body to help keep him or her warm. This method resembles the way a baby kangaroo snuggles inside their mother's pouch, which led to the term 'kangaroo care.' Research shows that kangaroo care can increase oxytocin and even decrease the risk of postpartum depression in mothers (Badr and Zauszniewski, 2017). Kangaroo care is common in NICU centers because, as it was explained to me by our

NICU nurse, the skin-to-skin contact has shown to help stabilize the premature baby's heart rate, breathing, regulate body temperature, and improve oxygen circulation. Research by Campbell-Yeo and colleagues also note positive effects on brain development (Campbell-Yeo, et al., 2015). For me, kangaroo care helped facilitate that bond with my baby. I felt more connected and relaxed when I held my baby in my arms. She was at peace and I was at peace. In addition to kangaroo care, there are other ways to increase oxytocin. Other types of physical touch, like gentle massage, or even eye contact have been shown to increase oxytocin levels as well.

Engage in Play Time Instead of Just 'Work' Time

There is so much involved with the day-to-day routine of early motherhood. For the baby, it's feeding baby, changing baby's diapers, changing baby's clothes, etc. But then there are things you need to do around the house to keep up with those things, like doing laundry so baby has clean clothes, making sure there are enough diapers and diaper cream, washing bottles and/or breast pump parts in the sink, for example. It can feel like there is a lot of 'work' time but little 'play' time. So, another easy way to bond with your baby is to set aside play time to have fun. Specifically, focus on spending time just being with your baby. Not because you *have* to, but because you *get* to. Play time in early infancy looks very different than toddler play time. In early infancy, play time might be singing to your baby or reading a book to your baby. It might mean letting your baby hold your finger while you make funny faces at them. It might mean putting a blanket down on the ground for 'tummy time' and showing little toys to your baby. It might mean putting your baby in a baby carrier and doing some slow rocking or dancing to music with them. I listened to music a lot with my baby. It's amazing how love songs on the radio can actually relate to other types of love instead of just romantic love. In fact, research has shown that soothing music can increase oxytocin levels as well (Nilsson, 2009).

Develop a Special Routine with Baby

Another way to develop a bond with your baby is to create a new routine or activity that you and your baby can engage in repeatedly. Something you can do repetitively, over and over again. Your routine could be a special outing or maybe just a stay-at-home activity. Even the simplest activities can develop into special routines. For me, I remember putting my baby in the stroller and walking to a local retail store. I would get myself a coffee drink and we would walk around the store, just hanging out. We got out of the house and it was 'our thing' that we did together. I also loved to make bath time a special routine for us. I would put my daughter in the tub and turn on music and sing songs to her while she splashed in the water. When I was cooking dinner, I would put her in a bounce chair so she could see everything I was doing, and I would pretend she was my audience for a cooking show. I would explain everything I was doing and she would watch me intently. There are so many routines we developed. For some ideas, look back on your routines or rituals you did growing up.

Obviously if you can remember them, you were older and not an infant, but maybe some of those routines can still be shared with your own baby.

Journal or Write Letters to Your Baby

I often encourage new mothers to journal or write letters to their baby. They write down what they love about their baby, the experiences they had together that day, or their hopes and dreams for the future. Some mothers have decided to write the journal in a way that they plan to give it to their baby when they are adults themselves. Or they decide to write letters to their baby to give to them when they are older. Some just write to help process their feelings and identify the small things they are grateful for, and never intend to let others read these letters. Taking the time to sit down and write something about your baby or to your baby can help you appreciate the details in the day and find joy in the little things you experience with your baby. It can easily shift perspective from feeling stressed and rushed to relaxed, focused, and more present.

Engage in Mindfulness with Baby

Another strategy to help facilitate the bond with your baby is engaging in the art of mindfulness. As mentioned before, it can feel as though the routine of early motherhood is a lot of work and little play. Mindfulness can help new mothers appreciate those little moments they have with baby, even during the 'work' moments. Mindfulness is increasing our awareness or focus to the present situation. A simple mindfulness technique would be going through your different senses during an activity you are engaging in with your baby. For example, you might be used to giving your baby a bath and just going through the motions. But it can help you bond and appreciate those 'motions' better when you are mindful. So, as you are giving your baby a bath, pay attention to everything you see. You might notice the bubbles in the bath, the way the water looks on your baby's skin, the way your baby splashes the water and shows curiosity toward it. Pay attention with your senses: what do you smell, hear, and feel? This technique can help you appreciate the 'work' moments much more. It can help you focus and stay present with your baby, which can help you facilitate your bond. No matter what you choose to do, or how you choose to facilitate the bond with your baby, making it a priority and focus of attention can be important for new moms.

Chapter 4

Practice #3: Secure Help and Support from Others

Offering help is courageous and compassionate, but so is asking for help.
– Brené Brown

As a psychologist, and simply a student of life, I have learned that we all need help sometimes. It doesn't matter if you are a single mom or if you have a partner in this journey, we all need help. This is hard for some people. It might be OK for us to ask for help finding something in the grocery store, but when it comes to *the most important job of raising children*, we somehow think we should do it all on our own? Huh? Of course, that doesn't make sense. But it is amazing how many new mothers think they should be able to do everything on their own. There is a reason why they say it 'takes a village' to raise a child. Being a new mom can feel very lonely and isolating at times. If there is one mistake that I see over and over again with new mothers I have worked with in therapy, is that they try to do everything on their own, without help. Maybe they feel afraid or embarrassed to ask for help or they just have that unrealistic expectation that they are *supposed* to do everything on their own. The problem is, that all new moms need a support system to help navigate through this journey.

When I met my husband, he was several years into his job as a mechanical engineer. His job required him to go to different power plants around the country and work for two to three months straight. I remember thinking, *this is going to be difficult for us as a couple to navigate this type of relationship.* Fast forward eight years later and he is still doing this type of work, even with two kids. As I am writing this now, my husband is six weeks into a three-month outage. His schedule is very demanding, so unfortunately, he is unable to come home during these work trips. That leaves me in charge of working full-time, raising our two children, and taking care of our dog. Needless to say, I would never be able to do this without my village. We moved to another state when my first daughter was an infant. We didn't have any family around, but luckily, we had good friends. I knew early on that my local support system was low, so I needed to build it up. After spending time focusing on expanding my support system, the next strategy was utilizing it and asking for help when I needed it. So, to simplify, there are two helpful steps: 1) Build your support system, and 2) Utilize it by reaching out and asking for help.

Build Your Support System

One of the first questions I always ask my new mother patients is what their support system looks like. Who is involved in their life? Who can they rely on and go to for support? Research shows that lower levels of social support increase a new mother's risk of developing postpartum depression (Corrigan, Kwasky, & Groh, 2015). This is why I always make a note of asking about the support system. A previous patient of mine, Rebecca, was a good example of this. When I first started working with her in therapy, it had been about 6 weeks since she had given birth. She and her husband had recently moved locations about three months into her pregnancy. They did not have any family or friends in the area. She said she knew it would be hard, but she could have never imagined it would be *this* hard. She was a stay-at-home mother with her son and felt very isolated. One of the first things we focused on was to increase her support system. Over the next few months, she increased her support system in several ways. She joined a church and started attending different church activities. She joined a new mom's group, where she and her son met up with other new moms and their children. She joined a new mom support group on Facebook. Later on, she joined one of those mommy-and-me music classes. She found several effective ways to meet new people. She said she would use any opportunity she could to meet new people. Even taking a walk with her baby and stopping to have a conversation with a neighbor was something she made a conscious effort to do as a way to meet people and form supportive relationships. As time went on, she began to really develop roots in her new community and decrease her isolation. As new moms, we don't have the time or energy to do everything on our own. We need help. It's OK to ask for help. It's OK to accept help. Not only is it OK but it's healthy! It can be a useful life skill. For example, in business, many successful people recognize when they need assistance with something: like learning from an expert in a specific field, delegating a project to another with more experience, accepting help from others who have been through a similar situation. These people are successful because they don't fall into the trap of doing everything on their own, which would lead them to feel overwhelmed, stressed, and frustrated. Well, a new mom is no different. In order to be successful and stay emotionally healthy, we also need to ask for help and accept help when needed.

I have seen many different groups for moms, including le Leche groups, mommy and baby yoga groups, new mother support groups, etc. These groups can be a great way to get support from others who are in similar situations. There can oftentimes be a sense of understanding when others go through similar experiences at the same time as you. Whether you join a specific type of mama group or you have supportive friends and family, it is important to utilize your support system during this time. Many times, our strength can come from others' support. There were many times after my daughter was born that I would feel refreshed, less discouraged, and more energized after meeting with other moms who were going through similar situations with their new babies.

Use Your Support System and Ask for Help

While it is important to build and expand your support system, it's not worth much if you don't use it. Many new moms fall into this trap, where they actually have a good support system, but they are too embarrassed or feel guilty about asking for help. I have to admit, I have fallen into this trap at times too. For me, I don't have the unrealistic expectation that I should do it on my own and I don't necessarily feel embarrassed about asking for help. For me, I can struggle with asking for help because I don't want to inconvenience or burden anyone. I know I need the help so I constantly challenge this thought. I have to remind myself that people want to help and others feel good when they can be helpful. I know I do. In fact, according to research, that is one of the keys to higher ratings of happiness: helping others. There are different kinds of support that new mothers need. Two of which, are physical and emotional support. An example of physical support is when I needed to call my friend to pick up my daughter from daycare because my car had been rear ended and I wasn't going to be at daycare in time before they closed. My friend was able to do something for me to help me out. In these cases, it can be helpful to be very specific about what kind of help you need. Honestly, for myself, sometimes I just wanted someone to watch the baby for a few hours so I could take a nap! Or take a shower. Or do something to relax. It can make a HUGE difference for a new mom to have some time to herself. When others would ask if they could help, I would practice saying, "Thank you for offering! I would love the help! What I really need right now is (insert helping behavior here). What day would work best for you?"

Figuring out what kind of help you need and specifically asking for it can be useful.

Another example of support would be emotional support. These are the things that others can do that help you out emotionally. For example, I had a close friend who would drop by my house every weekend when my husband was out of town to listen to me when I needed to vent or just simply have an adult conversation. My neighbors would constantly ask if I needed help and honestly just having a conversation where they listened was helpful a lot of the time! The beauty of emotional support is that you don't need to be with the person to get this type of support. I would talk to family members on the phone and it would mean the world to me to hear, 'You got this.' I remember calling friends and simply asking for parenting advice about this or that. I learned a lot from my other mom friends. One of my common coping skills for navigating the process of being a new mom, was asking LOTS of questions and gathering information from other moms. Asking your own mom, a sister, a friend or mentor questions about their experiences. Most likely, they have been through something similar. As a new mom you will have tons of questions. There is no way around it. And as I mentioned before, people like to help! It can also help others feel more confident in their own mothering skills, like "Hey, I actually know something here!" Sometimes I would follow others' advice but sometimes I wouldn't. Sometimes what is right for one person isn't necessarily right for another. But just having these conversations was supportive for me. Having both emotional and physical supports are necessary at different times during the early motherhood process.

I would encourage new moms to ask themselves, "What gets in the way of me asking others for help?" If it is the unrealistic expectation that you are supposed to do everything on your own, then you need to challenge that expectation. Reminding yourself that it is not a weakness to ask for help, but rather a sign of courage. Reminding yourself that in other countries and cultures, it is common for family and friends to play an active role in the postpartum process. If you are embarrassed because you think others might judge you or if you feel guilty about burdening others, then again, you need to challenge these thoughts. Following these steps of building your support system and utilizing it is a necessary part of adjusting to motherhood.

Chapter 5

Practice #4: Identify and Change Problematic Self-Talk

> *Whether you think you can*
> *or you can't, you're right.*
> – Henry Ford

The psychologist in me loves this quote. It pretty much sums up how powerful our thoughts and self-talk can be. Many people struggle with problematic self-talk, and new mothers are no exception. As discussed earlier in the book, our self-talk includes thoughts that we have about ourselves or messages we might tell ourselves. We don't necessarily always say these things to ourselves out loud. An example might be if we think to ourselves, *Oh man, I really stink at this parenting thing.* Usually, we aren't even aware of our thoughts and the judgments we put on ourselves. The biggest problem with using problematic self-talk, however, is that it can affect our emotions and behaviors in a very negative way. This is one of the underlying bases of cognitive-behavioral therapy, which is one of the most researched and commonly used theoretical orientations by therapists.

To put it simply, there is a relationship between our cognitions/thoughts, emotions/feelings, and behaviors. So, the way we think affects how we feel and how we behave. For example, if you have the thought, *Oh man, I really stink at this parenting thing*, this might make you feel sad, discouraged, or frustrated. This may also affect your behaviors and what you do. You might lash out and yell at your husband or you might engage in unhealthy coping strategies. So, it can be helpful to identify problematic self-talk and replace it. To keep it simple, think of there being two steps in this process: *identify* and *change*.

Identify Problematic Self-Talk

Identifying problematic self-talk is the first necessary step. However, it's not that easy. As I said earlier, a lot of our self-talk we are not even aware of, which makes it difficult to identify. Sometimes it helps to notice your feeling first and then work backward. To first notice when you are feeling sad, discouraged, or frustrated, and to ask yourself, why do I feel this way? What happened? What am I telling or saying to myself about this situation? One way to identify problematic self-talk is to watch out for cognitive distortions. Below are some common cognitive distortions:

1. Filtering: focusing on the negative aspects of a situation.
2. All or nothing thinking: viewing a situation as one way or another with nothing in between.
3. Catastrophizing: blowing a situation out of proportion in a negative direction.

4. 'Should' statements: telling yourself you 'should' do something in a situation, which can elicit blame and guilt.

Here is an example of negative self-talk using the above cognitive distortions:

I'm feeling so frustrated. All day, I clean up poop and spit up and listen to crying (filtering). This day has completely stunk (all or nothing thinking). I'm obviously a horrible mom and can't take care of a baby. Clearly, I'm screwing up this poor baby for years to come (catastrophizing). I should be better at this ('should' statement).

As a new mom, when you are giving yourself these negative messages, it is likely you may feel pretty bad about yourself and your abilities as a mother. So, identifying our negative thoughts in the first place is an important step. Again, one way to identify our negative self-talk is to notice how we are feeling and what messages we are telling ourselves related to our situation. So, to simplify: the first step is to identify, the second step is to change. This brings us to step two…

Change Problematic Self-Talk

Once we become aware that we are engaging in negative or problematic self-talk, then we can do something about it. Sometimes to change our negative mindset, we can engage in coping skills to help us reset (fast forward to

Chapter 6). But we can also change our negative self-talk or 'stinkin' thinkin' as many CBT enthusiasts would say. One way we could challenge our self-talk is by examining the evidence by looking for the exception. For example, instead of telling yourself, this day has completely stunk. I obviously am a horrible mom and can't take care of a baby right…you can challenge this by looking for the exception. Instead focusing on, OK, this day hasn't been all bad. We had such a fun time at the park today…or…OK, I'm obviously not a horrible mom. I do so many things well… This helps you shift your focus from a negative to a more realistic viewpoint. Maybe a more balanced and realistic thought is that while you will struggle with some things as a parent (like we all do), you will also do many things well. When we only focus on the negative, we tend to only see one side of things. Many times, it's better to focus on the whole picture. When we look at a situation from a more realistic lens instead of a negative lens, this can affect how we feel about a situation.

Let's say you are struggling with calming your baby. He is crying, uncontrollably and can't seem to be comforted. This one piece of evidence might lead one to say to themselves, "I can't seem to do this parenting thing right." You are focusing on this one negative piece of evidence to come up with your conclusion that you can't do this parenting thing right. A way to challenge this problematic self-talk is to examine ALL the evidence before coming to a conclusion. To find other evidence, ask yourself, what are some things that I do well as a parent? When have I felt like I knew something about this parenting thing? What about all those other times when I successfully was able to calm my baby? When you look at all the evidence, most likely you will make a more accurate conclusion. Maybe a more realistic thought is, Like all parents, sometimes I struggle with this parenting thing but I have learned a lot and there are many things that I do well as a parent.

Another strategy to help challenge our negative self-talk is to identify double standards. In other words, identify when you are treating yourself more negatively or harshly than you would treat a friend in the same situation. For example, you get the baby ready, pack up the diaper bag, put the baby in the car, and start driving to the park. You realize halfway to the park that you forgot to put the diaper bag in the car. You might say to yourself, "Ugh, I'm so stupid. I can't believe I forgot that." But would you talk that way to your friend in the same situation? Doubtful. You would probably be more supportive. Talking to yourself the way you would talk to a friend in the same situation is a good way to challenge negative self-talk. Practicing self-compassion can be a useful tool not only in early motherhood but throughout your lifetime.

Another good way to challenge negative self-talk is to use positive affirmations. Positive affirmations can be simple sentences or phrases you can say or read to yourself. Positive affirmations can be powerful. Examples of parenting specific positive affirmations might be:

- You are a good mother.
- You love and care for our baby.
- You want the best for your baby.
- You have many great qualities.
- You do so many things right as a mom.

- You are learning to recognize cues from your baby.
- It's OK to make some mistakes as a parent.
- It's OK to have doubts and fears as a parent.
- You are learning how to adjust your roles as a mother, partner, friend, etc.

But even non-specific parenting positive affirmations are helpful, like:

- You've got this.
- I can do this.
- I believe in you.
- You are strong.

When moms are really struggling with their self-talk, I will oftentimes suggest that they make a list of positive affirmations they can use whenever they need to. It can be helpful to use these affirmations throughout the day, to help change any problematic self-talk and to shift the focus to look at the whole picture instead of filtering. Some moms keep a list in their purse or diaper bag and pull it out to use as a coping strategy. Some post it on their bathroom wall and read them whenever they see it. Some choose one affirmation each day and repeat it throughout the day like a mantra. Whatever you choose to do, it can be helpful to remind yourself of these positive things on a frequent basis.

Another way to challenge negative self-talk is to reduce using 'should' statements. When we use 'should' statements, we can put a sense of pressure or blame on ourselves for our actions. Common 'should' statements might be:

1. I should be happier with my baby.
2. I should be able to care for my baby by myself.
3. I should never get frustrated.
4. I should know what I'm doing without asking for help.
5. I should be a better mother, partner, etc.

When we use 'should' statements, we might believe we are not living up to these standards. We might feel judged that others expect these things from us too. We might feel anxious or exhausted, since these 'should' statements can put a lot of pressure on a person. Overall, there are many useful tools we can use to help identify and change our negative self-talk. Practicing healthy self-talk and being compassionate with ourselves is important in early motherhood and afterward.

Chapter 6

Practice #5: Learn to Incorporate Self-Care Strategies

Self-care is giving the world the best of you,
instead of what's left of you.
– Katie Reed

Many new moms might laugh at the idea of self-care. I mean, after all, who has time for it? In the blink of an eye, we have a new baby to take care of that demands the large majority of our time and attention. We only have so many minutes in a day. When something demands more of our time, we tend to drop other time-sucking things off at the wayside. Self-care oftentimes moves to the lower end of the priority list, to free up time and energy for caring for baby. However, this strategy tends to be a problem for many new mothers. We use all our energy throughout the day taking care of others, completing tasks, etc. We are completely drained by the end of the day. Self-care is a way to recharge our battery so we are not constantly depleted and running on empty. This way, you can give others the best of you. A lot of the time what happens when our stress levels rise, is that our self-care decreases. Again, part of it is that we are so focused on dealing with whatever the stressor is, that we feel as though we don't have time for self-care. However, the reality is that under times of increased stress, self-care should be more of a priority as a way to help us cope and deal more effectively with the stressor. And having a baby is a new stressor. A wonderful stressor, but a stressor none the less. According to the Holmes and Rahe Stress Scale, pregnancy and gain of a new family member rank within the top 15 stressors that a person can go through at a given time (Holmes and Rahe, 1967). Even great things in our life (i.e., getting married, vacation, and Christmas) are on the list because they still add some amount of stress to our lives. Taking care of ourselves and our needs is essential for new moms. Because, as my friend Kelly says, "If mama's good, then baby's good."

Find Self-Care Strategies

So, the obvious first step is to find self-care strategies. Maybe you already know which skills work for you, but you just need to make self-care a priority and set aside time to use these skills. Or maybe you don't have a lot of self-care skills and you need to explore new skills. Either way, the goal is to put many tools in your toolbox. Having a variety of self-care strategies can be useful. Basically, a self-care skill is something you can do that decreases your stress level and recharges your battery. Some self-care strategies can be more time consuming than others, and having both longer and shorter timed skills can be good to add to your toolbox. For example, scheduling a Pamper Day (and no I don't mean diapers) like getting a massage can be a wonderful way to decrease stress; however, it might not be something we can do all that often. Other great self-care strategies include exercise, yoga, or meditation/prayer. Some shorter and easier skills might be learning guided imagery, mindfulness, journaling, progressive muscle relaxation, or deep breathing. Finding skills that you can use within five minutes is just as necessary. The internet has tons of resources for guided imagery, meditations, etc. Also, there are more specific self-care skills on The Resilient New Mom webpage at www.theresilientnewmom.com that can help you walk through specific skills. For some, watching a funny movie where you laugh can definitely lead to relaxation. The Facial Feedback Hypothesis suggests that just the act of smiling can affect one's emotional state in a positive way. Having a hard time finding something that makes you laugh? Search on the internet: 'laughing therapy' or 'laughing yoga' and watch a video of a bunch of people sitting around laughing. You can't help but not laugh.

It is also important to focus on basic needs. Even the more simplistic needs are important to meet. Maslow's Hierarchy of Needs illustrates nicely how physiological needs should be an important focus. These needs might include focusing on eating healthy, nutritious food and getting rest and sleep. I cannot tell you how many new mothers struggle with getting their basic physiological needs met. They don't have time to eat full meals but rather just find snacks when they have a few quick minutes. And sleep? That's a whole separate book. But one piece of friendly advice is to try to get some chunks of sleep whenever possible. Sometimes that might entail someone else looking over the baby so there can be some amount of time where there is undisturbed sleep. I've had many new mom clients walk into our therapy session where they were emotionally and physically exhausted. I always ask about basic needs of eating and sleeping and that's oftentimes the first place of focus during the session.

Set Realistic Goals and Implement

Now that we've gone over some ideas of what self-care can look like, it's just as important to set realistic goals for self-care. When it comes to implementing self-care, focus on quality over quantity. Many new moms can fall into the trap of all or nothing thinking when it comes to self-care. In other words, it's important to remember that you don't have to do everything or nothing. There is a lot of space in between. For example, with self-care, it's probably not realistic that you spend four hours a day on self-care. I have not met a new mom who can dedicate that much time to self-care. But even finding five minutes in the beginning of your day for deep breathing or meditation can be helpful. Or ten minutes at the end of the day to journal. Or taking baby for a walk outside to get some exercise can be useful. It may be necessary to set aside a specific time during your day for regularly engaging in self-care AND to use self-care strategies when you are noticing that you need to. For example, I usually promote doing 'stress check-ins' throughout the day to see whether you may need to utilize some coping skills. Asking yourself on a scale of 1–10, with 1 being very little stress and 10 being extreme stress, where do I fall right now? Am I irritated? Are my muscles tight? These questions can help you become aware of your degree of stress or tension. If you notice yourself creeping up on the scale, then it's a good time to engage in self-care, even for a few minutes. When our stress increases, our sympathetic nervous system gears up our physiological responses. We might begin to breathe shallower, our muscles become tighter, etc. Deep breathing can help activate our parasympathetic nervous system, which helps us relax. This can be a very useful skill to practice. A common activity I encourage is to make self-care as easy as possible by creating a self-care box. Find a box where you might put in a scented candle or lotion for aromatherapy, a journal and pen, a favorite playlist with relaxing music, a DVD of your favorite yoga video, a travel magazine or favorite book, a good packet of tea, a list with inspiring quotes or messages, etc. As with any new skill we learn, learning new coping skills requires practice before we get good at it. It often takes time to learn how to use these skills regularly and for them to be effective. For those of you who are visual people, creating a self-care chart can be useful which lists your common self-care strategies. As new moms, it's hard to put our best foot forward when we are tired, depleted, or exhausted. We cannot be as effective if we feel as though we are consistently running on fumes. Finding ways to recharge your battery and reenergize yourself can help make the transition to motherhood a little easier.

Chapter 7

Practice #6: Incorporate All Parts of Your Identity

Individuality is very important for a full human life.
– Dalai Lama

New mothers can struggle with the transition into motherhood for many reasons, but one of those reasons may be due to feeling a loss in themselves as an individual. While they have gained this new role as a mother, they may feel some loss in their personal identity or who they were before their baby was born. There has been a change, and with change oftentimes comes some loss of how something used to be. For some new moms, they feel their sense of self has changed. A very new and major role now is that of being a mother. While this is an important role, it is not our *only* role. Many times, in order for us to be good moms, we need to include all parts of our identity into our lives. Even very positive changes, like getting married, can cause us to give up things. For example, you may lose some sense of freedom or you may need to give up things being 'your way.' This is common. When it comes to being a new parent, I have seen many new mothers struggle because they have let go of those parts of themselves that helped fulfill them. They sometimes struggle with grieving the loss of their 'old' self. But what's important to remember, is that we can include parts of our 'old' self into our new situation. In other words, we can learn to incorporate all parts of our identity and continue to focus on all parts of ourselves that make us who we are and help fulfill us. Instead of replacing a previous part, we can just add another. When we make this our goal, this may help create a better sense of balance or adjustment. There is this faulty belief out there that mothers are supposed to drop everything when they become a mom and solely immerse themselves in their new role. If this works for you, then great. But for many new mothers, this strategy doesn't work and they feel better when all parts of their identity are integrated.

What Is Personal Identity?

When I refer to personal identity, I'm referring to all the parts of you who make up who you are as a person. In adulthood, we have so many roles. As we get older, we seem to add more and more roles to our identities. Early in our adult life, we add the role of being an employer or worker. If you get married or are in a relationship, you may have the role of a partner. When you become a parent, a new role is that of being a mother or father. As I sit here and think about it, I am aware of many roles that are attached to my identity and different parts of myself that help make me the person that I am. Obviously, a big role for me is being a mom. But I have other parts of me that are important to me and help make up who I am. For example, I am a wife. I am a friend. I am a psychologist. I am a writer. I am a (skier, tennis player, runner, swimmer, or insert any of my physical activities here). I am a travel lover. And the list goes on. There are many different parts of me who make me the person I am. Being a mother is one of the most important of those roles, but there are also other things that are part of me and my life that make me happy and help me feel fulfilled. When we begin to neglect important parts of ourselves, we might begin to feel unbalanced or even unhappy. It can be helpful to incorporate all parts of our identity.

I love being a mother. I love my kids. But I know I am a better mother and my kids ultimately benefit when I focus on incorporating all parts of my identity. For me, writing this book gave me a good outlet to focus on several different parts of myself that are important to me: being a psychologist and a writer. When we make motherhood our only role, we might start to feel burned out. This might lead to feeling resentful, irritable, or unhappy. Learning to incorporate all parts of our identity can be helpful.

Identify and Incorporate All Parts of Your Identity

The first step with this practice is to first identify the different parts of yourself that make up who you are. It can be a useful activity to get out a piece of paper and write down all of the roles that contribute to who you are as a person. Ask yourself, what are my roles? What do I love to do? What am I passionate about? What are my hobbies and interests? What helps fulfill me as a person? When I am at my best, what am I doing or incorporating into my life? What are my goals? My focuses? These questions can help you identify the differing aspects of your personal identity that contribute to who you are as a person. Once you are able to clarify the parts of your personal identity, you can then find specific ways to include them into your life. For some moms, it might be continuing a past hobby or interest. One of my friends is an avid runner. After she had her first baby, she gave up race training. She missed it. It was a huge part of who she was. It impassioned her. She was able to recognize how important this part of herself was and she eventually signed up for a race again. Continuing to engage in those activities or roles that make you who you are can be essential. Maybe you won't be able to engage in these activities or roles in the same frequency as you did before you had kids, but that's OK and you won't need to. A 'balance' won't mean 'even' in this case. But as I work with new moms, a little focus in these other areas can go a long way. Learning to incorporate all parts of your identity can help ease the transition into motherhood. Instead of feeling as though you are giving up or losing part of who you are, you can begin to realize that you are actually adding a new and exciting role as mother to the already established parts that make up who you are.

Chapter 8

Practice #7: Evolve Your Relationship with Your Partner

The greatest gift a couple can give their baby is a loving relationship, because that relationship nourishes Baby's development. The stronger the connection between parents, the healthier the child can grow, both emotionally and intellectually.
– John M. Gottman

When I first started working with Natalie in therapy, her son was five months old. During the session, she frequently smiled while she talked and overall, she had a very bubbly personality. On the surface, she appeared as though she had everything figured out. However, as we got further into our first session and the layers of Natalie slowly began peeling away, I recognized that she was really struggling. She was exhausted and overwhelmed. Her relationship with her husband, John, was on shaky ground. They didn't spend much time focusing on their relationship as a couple anymore. They argued more frequently and her satisfaction in her relationship was low. She felt as though she was taking care of all her baby's needs, with little help from her husband. She became bitter, easily frustrated, and resentful in the relationship. Because of her resentment, she recognized she would find any excuse to start an argument with him. She wanted to make his life just as miserable as how she felt inside. She assumed that if she brought up her frustration with him, then he would just change, right? Unfortunately, that's not what happened. When she brought up her frustrations with her husband, he oftentimes would get defensive. She admitted that she tended to bring up her frustrations in an aggressive manner, since she was very angry. This, however, would cause her husband to try to defend himself. While many of her frustrations were valid, unfortunately her message would get lost because of how it was delivered. These frequent exchanges between the two of them helped pave the way for more toxicity and resentment to grow between them. They were stuck in this resentment trap. Her husband's way of dealing with Natalie, was to avoid her, which only made Natalie more upset and frustrated.

Natalie wasn't the only new mom who noticed more struggles in her relationship with her partner soon after a baby was born. According to Gottman and Silver (1999), 70% of wives experience a plummet in their marital satisfaction in the year after the first baby arrives. This is in part due to a distance that can grow between the partners if both parents fail to move forward with the transition into parenthood. In Natalie's case, communication in her relationship had gone awry. After regularly participating in therapy over the next several months, however, this troublesome dynamic and pattern began to change for the better. Among other things, we focused on evolving her relationship with her husband. So, what are some helpful tools couples can focus on?

Focus on Working Together Toward a Goal

From Natalie's point of view, her husband did not do enough around the house. The baby's laundry was piling up. The grocery shopping list kept getting longer and longer. The floor needed to be swept. Natalie would get so frustrated with her husband for not initiating the completion of these tasks. Finally, after her frustration mounted, she said she would 'blow up' and yell at him to complete one of these tasks. When she brought it up to him, he would do it, but he would get angry at her for being 'rude' and 'naggy'. After months of this dynamic, we were discussing this unfortunate pattern in my office. She said, "It's so frustrating! When I get home from work, I walk in the door and notice the dust on the TV stand, crumbs in the corner of the kitchen, and leftovers in the fridge that need to be thrown out. I get so angry that he doesn't take the initiative and help out! I shouldn't have to ask him to do these things! He should just do them on his own. Doesn't he see it!" But Natalie began to realize that maybe he didn't see it. She began to recognize that just because she noticed these things and they were a priority for her, it didn't mean that her husband noticed them or that they were a priority for him. We talked about how we each have strengths and weaknesses, and they vary from person to person. Instead of focusing on how frustrating their differences were, the real question became: *How do we work together in a way that capitalizes on our strengths?* Only until that became their new focus, were Natalie and her husband able to successfully manage their strengths and weaknesses and develop a strategy for moving forward. Natalie and her husband began creating a mutual list of tasks to complete. Then they worked on splitting up the tasks between the two of them. It's not necessarily a problem that there are differences between partners, but what is important is how couples deal with and manage those differences by working together as a team, instead of against each other. When Natalie and her husband came up with a plan to manage their differences and work on their goal, it helped change their relationship. For them, instead of getting lost in the problem, they began to focus on a solution.

Discuss Expectations of Parenting

One of the most important things that new parents can do, is to have a conversation about expectations and shared roles/responsibilities of parenthood. Openly communicating these things can help clarify expectations and responsibilities. Sometimes when these things are not discussed, they can be a source of argument between partners. Whether you are still waiting for your baby to arrive or you are in the beginning throws of motherhood, having a conversation about being parents as well as the tasks involved with parenting will be important. This way, couples can openly communicate their own expectations, roles, and responsibilities to help facilitate both parents moving forward. So, what questions could be explored by the couple? Below are some ideas that may be beneficial to discuss with each other about parenting:

- How do I feel about being a parent?
- What am I most looking forward to about being a parent?
- What I am most nervous about with being a parent?
- What do I think might be one of the most challenging parts of being a new parent?
- How can we work together to try to overcome these possible challenges?
- What was modeled to me by my parents regarding the differing roles in parenting? Is that how I picture our roles to be?
- How will we break up the specific tasks involved with being a new parent? (i.e., feedings, diaper changes, baths, etc.)

There is not necessarily a right and wrong answer to these questions. The most important thing is to open the lines of communication to make sure your views are discussed. Obviously, things will likely change and you need to be flexible, but having an initial conversation can help clarify expectations and will also help both parties move forward. Eventually, Natalie and her husband were able to discuss these questions to open the lines of communication between them. Any differences they had; they were able to create a plan to work through their differences.

Have Frequent Check-Ins

These parenting prep conversations, however, are not necessarily a one-time thing. Many couples like to check in with each frequently to discuss what is working and what is not working for them. This way, adjustments can be made. It can be helpful to talk about what is going well in addition to ways you can alter the things that are not working. Example questions to check in could be:

- What is going well for us?
- What isn't working so well for us?
- What could we change to make things better?

These frequent conversations can help avoid the buildup of resentment from holding in frustrations, as they did in Natalie's case. Talking about expectations, roles, and responsibilities regularly by using assertive communication can help reduce resentment. One way to think about the buildup of resentment is to imagine a soda bottle. When it gets shaken up, it's important to let the air out slowly so it doesn't explode. Same thing with resentment. When problems arise, it's important to discuss them before the resentment continues to grow in order to prevent the explosive argument that can follow.

A good way to discuss problems or concerns is to use assertive communication techniques. The easiest example of an assertive communication statement is:

"I feel – because –"

Following up your assertive communication statement with a solution might be a good next sentence. That way, as discussed above, instead of focusing on the problem you offer a solution. So, a basic sentence would be:

"I feel (insert emotion) **because** (insert problem). **I was thinking maybe** *we* **could** (insert solution) **to see if that works better."**

Notice how the wording is 'we.' These creates a team approach that helps both parties feel like they are working together toward something instead of against each other.

Have you heard the phrase, "It's not what you say, but how you say it?" In many situations, the way you say something can make a big difference in how the message is received. Oftentimes, if you bring up a problem in an accusatory way, the other person automatically becomes defensive and feels the need to defend themselves. When this happens, the message can easily get lost. In order to try to prevent defensiveness from entering the conversation, using the assertive communication technique discussed above can help. Let's take Natalie's case for example. She would oftentimes say things to her husband like, "You never wash the baby's laundry! I'm always the one cleaning! What's wrong with you!" These types of responses didn't work out well for Natalie because her husband would feel attacked. This would usually put him on the defensive, which in turn would escalate the conversation. When this happens, the original message gets lost and nobody wins. Instead, Natalie practiced the assertive communication technique of:

"I feel _(insert emotion)___ **because** _(insert problem).
I was thinking maybe *we* **could** (insert solution)____ **to see if that works better."**

For example, she could say something like,

"I feel overwhelmed **because** there is so much of the baby's laundry to do. **I was thinking maybe** *we* **could**

switch off doing the baby's laundry **to see if that works better."**

This type of statement brings up a specific problem and offers a solution. The partner is less likely to get defensive, which allows the message to be heard and dealt with accordingly.

Dedicate Time for Your Relationship with Your Partner

In order to help both partners move forward through the transition into parenthood together, it can be helpful to dedicate specific time to spend on the relationship. Many of you might be thinking to yourself, *Dedicate time to my relationship?!?! When would I be able to do that with all the other stuff I have to do as a new mom?!?!* While you likely will not be able to dedicate as much time as you could before the baby was born, even if you can find a couple of hours a week, that would be beneficial. Your idea of a 'date night' most likely will change. The things you used to do during your time together might look different now. But that's OK. As we saw in Natalie's case, she and her husband did not put in much time toward their relationship and the focus was mostly on taking care of their son and the household duties. Before their baby was born, they had a 'date night' in which they would try out a new restaurant in their city every Thursday. After their son was born, however, they were not able to do that as often as they could. So, they didn't do anything. Eventually, after eight months they began to incorporate their weekly date nights back into their routine; but instead, they brought the restaurant to their house! They would order food in from a new restaurant one night a week after they put the baby to bed. Or they would try a new recipe that they cooked together. They changed their traditional date night and replaced it with another routine that allowed them to spend time together, which allowed them to focus on one another and their relationship. They adapted together and their relationship evolved as a result.

Maybe your time with your partner will look different than Natalie and her husband's. For you, it might be a movie night where you rent a movie to watch at home and make popcorn. Maybe it's a game night where you play cards or board games with your partner. It doesn't matter as much what you do, but rather that you spend some time dedicated to your relationship. As Gottman and Silver mention, it is not necessarily helpful to view marriage and family as a 'balancing act.' It is oftentimes unrealistic for parents to spend as much time on their relationship as on their new baby. But even some focus can be a breath of fresh air. The most important thing is that partners make the transition forward together. Yes, you may not be able to do the things you once could in your relationship as frequently as you used to. But you can still incorporate some of those things into your relationship or find new things to do together to evolve your relationship.

Don't Get Stuck in the Filtering Funk

Many times, when resentment builds, partners tend to focus on the negative and what their partner doesn't do, as we saw in Natalie's case. It is important to also focus on what they do right. Filtering is when we focus on the negatives and ignore the positives. When we filter and only focus on the negatives, this can make us feel depressed, frustrated, or full or resentment. We get stuck in the Filtering Funk. When this happens, it can be helpful to focus on what your partner does well.

For example, Natalie felt like she was the one doing most of the tasks around the house. Natalie, however, would oftentimes engage in filtering and focus on what her husband did wrong. She was hoping to change his behavior by yelling at him to help out more around the house. Obviously, this didn't work. She began to focus on avoiding the Filtering Funk by reminding herself of all of the things that her husband does well. Instead of focusing on what he does wrong, she would focus on positive ways her husband contributed. She would catch him when he was putting the dishes away and thank him for doing so. She would catch him when he took out the garbage and tell him how much she appreciated his help. This positive reinforcement worked well. By focusing on the ways her husband was contributing, it helped with Natalie's frustration and helped her husband feel more appreciated, which also helped improve their relationship.

Learn a Way to Let Go

In a relationship, it is important to find ways to 'let go.' Let go of the anger, let go of the frustration, let go of the resentment. If we have difficulty in letting go of these things, we oftentimes carry it with us into the next argument. To help let go of the anger, ask yourself, "Am I going to care about this in a week? In a month? In a year?" Most of the time, the answer is no. How many times can you look back on an argument you had with a partner and you have no idea what you were arguing about? Most of the time, we might care in the moment but later we recognize that it may have not been as big of a deal as we originally thought.

Another simple way of letting go might be to journal or write it down. I'm a firm believer that we oftentimes get 'stuck' in our heads when we ruminate about something over and over again. But writing it down or talking about it helps us get 'unstuck' by allowing our brains to process the information differently. This process can help us make better sense of our emotions and also allow us to think about things more rationally.

Bringing a new baby into the world incorporates a whole new set of challenges and feelings. Many things change as a result, including your relationship with your partner. To help successfully transition through this new period, it is important to continue to evolve your relationship with your partner and focus on ways to work together through the transition. It is also important to learn ways to navigate difficult parenting moments, which brings us to our next chapter...

Chapter 9

Practice #8: Navigate SOS Mommy Moments: Ways to Manage Feelings When Overwhelmed

The joy of motherhood comes in moments. There will be hard times and frustrating times.
But amid the challenges, there are shining moments of joy and satisfaction.
– Elder M. Russell Ballard

All new mothers have been there before. Those days when nothing seems to be going right. Those days when you can't catch a break and you are beyond frustrated. Those days when your baby has been crying for what feels like forever and you can't get him or her to stop. Those days when you can't seem to get your little one to sleep and you are exhausted. As new mothers, we've all had *those days* when we feel like our limit has been reached and our threshold is crossed. When we are so frustrated, irritable, anxious, and overwhelmed that we don't know how we are going to get through another second. These are what I call SOS Mommy Moments. You may have heard the term SOS before. SOS in Morse code is a 'signal' indicating distress and the need for help. SOS Mommy Moments are those times in mommyhood when you are feeling in complete distress and need help.

When I was a new mother, I also had my fair share of SOS Mommy Moments. However, looking back on my own SOS Mommy Moments, they don't seem like such a big deal anymore. But in the moment, I remembering feeling like I was losing an endless battle. Sometimes an SOS Mommy Moment happens when some one major thing goes wrong. Other times it's more of a buildup where multiple minor things are adding up and you encounter the 'last straw' problem that puts you over the edge. In these SOS Mommy Moments, when you're at your wits end, it's important to learn ways to tolerate or cope with distress in the moment. Below are strategies to help navigate these SOS Mommy Moments.

Take a 'Time Out'

Some parents use the 'time out' approach with their children as a way of modifying behavior. Some people view time outs as a form of punishment for their children when they are behaving badly. However, other parents look at the time out as a way to help their children learn the importance of taking time away from distractions to help regroup and calm themselves. When we view time outs in that way, even adults (especially new moms) can benefit big time from this approach. When you are in an SOS Mommy Moment and you have reached your limit, one of the best things you can do is find a way to regroup, both emotionally and physically. Sometimes just taking a minute or two can make a big difference in your ability to cope with distress. Call in the reinforcements if you need to. If you are able to, tag out and let your partner take over. If not, it's OK to give yourself permission to let the baby briefly cry in a safe place while you take a few moments to regroup. There are many things you can do during your mommy time out. Below are examples of things you can do during this time. Whatever you choose to do, however, the goal should be to calm yourself and regroup.

Be Your Own Cheerleader

Many times, when we are in an SOS Mommy Moment, our self-talk becomes very negative. We oftentimes are critical of ourselves and our situations. Some common examples of negative self-talk that I commonly hear new moms say during SOS Mommy Moments:

- I can't do this!
- This will never get better!
- I am the worst mom ever!
- Nothing is working!

The problem with this type of self-talk, is that it can oftentimes exacerbate our feelings of frustration, anxiety, and anger. We want our situation to improve, yet our negative self-talk oftentimes adds fuel to the fire of negativity. Instead, it is helpful in these moments to focus on using positive self-talk that will in turn help reduce feelings of frustration, anxiety, anger, etc. One way to do this, is to Be Your Own Cheerleader. In these situations, it can be helpful to talk to yourself as if you were talking to a friend who was struggling. What would you say to them? What would you want to hear others say to you in this moment? Here are some examples of things I would say to myself in these moments:

- Katie, you can do this!
- This will end! It cannot last forever.
- Katie, you are a good mom.
- Katie, you've been through worse before.
- Just breathe. You will be OK.

You may be noticing that the 'I' statements, have been replaced with my first name. The reason for this, comes from research by Ethan et al. These researchers found that how people conduct their inner monologues has a large effect on their success. If you talk to yourself with the pronoun *I*, for instance, you may be likely to fluster and perform poorly in stressful circumstances. Instead, if you address yourself by your name, you are more likely to succeed in a variety of situations. By changing the way, we address ourselves (i.e., first person or third person) we flip switches in the cerebral cortex and the amygdala, which helps us create a distance from the emotionality of ourselves. Gaining psychological distance allows us to gain more self-control, think clearly, and perform more successfully.

Learn Deep Breathing

One of the easiest ways to navigate SOS Mommy Moments is to focus on your breathing. When we are in the middle of an SOS Mommy Moment, oftentimes our 'fight or flight' response is activated. Dr. Herbert Benson wrote in The Relaxation Response (1992) that humans react to stress on an emotional and physical level. The 'fight or flight' response is a common term used to describe the effects that stress has on the body. Our fight or flight response is regulated by our sympathetic nervous system and important for our survival from an evolutionary perspective. When we are feeling stressed, our muscles tense. Our breathing becomes more rapid and shallow and we are not getting enough oxygen into our bodies. Our heart beats faster. We begin to sweat. Unfortunately, sometimes our 'fight or flight' system kicks in when we don't necessarily want it to. When this happens, it is helpful to find a way to release tension and relax. That's where deep breathing comes in. When we engage in deep breathing, we begin to take in long, slower breaths. That helps communicate to our body to relax and calm. Our bodies start to recognize that there is no threat and we are safe. When we begin to change our breathing, we then begin to notice our other physiological responses follow. Our heart rate begins to decrease. Our muscles start to relax. This is the basic description of how deep breathing works. Deep breathing can be used as a muscle relaxer by helping release tension in the muscles.

To start, begin to breathe in through your nose and out your mouth. The first step in deep breathing is to be aware of the breathing process. Notice the breath as it enters your nose and as it exits your body. Slow inhales and slow exhales. With every exhale, focus on letting go of the tension in your body. Maybe you hold the tension in your neck, shoulders, back, or face. As you are breathing out, work on releasing the tension in those areas. Some people only focus on the breath during deep breathing. Others add a mantra into the process, like 'release' or 'calm.' Continue breathing like this for several minutes. As you continue to breathe, you may notice that your heart rate begins to decrease, your muscles begin to relax more, and you feel calmer. The nice thing about using deep breathing as a coping skill, is that you can use it anywhere. Focusing on taking long, deep breaths during Mommy SOS Situations can help you navigate the struggle. Even if you bring the level of stress and tension from a 9 out of 10 to a 6 out of 10, that is progress and beneficial to help you get through the moment.

Create an SOS Mommy Mantra

When people think of the word 'mantra,' they oftentimes think of a word or phrase that is repeated often with the intent of bringing focus to the word or phrase while reducing focus on stimuli around us. A mantra allows us to focus on a single thought or idea, which helps prevent distraction from other thoughts and emotions. When you are having an SOS Mommy Moment, it is easy to get caught up in the distractions around us, or even the distractions in our own mind. Shifting your focus to a mommy mantra can help you disregard those distractions by shifting your focus elsewhere. Here are some helpful examples of mantras:

- Release things out of my control
- Let it go
- Find calm in the storm
- Accept the things that cannot be changed
- What doesn't kill you makes you stronger
- If I think I can, I'm right. If I think I can't, I'm right
- All days end. Tomorrow is a new day
- This too shall pass
- Breathe
- I will survive
- Love is all you need

Having a mantra to focus on allows you to focus on a single thought or idea, which in turn will help prevent distraction from other thoughts and emotions that frequently occur in SOS Mommy Moments.

Put Yourself in Your Baby's 'Booties'

During an SOS Mommy Moment, we can easily become frustrated not only with ourselves and our situation but with our baby too. In order to reduce our frustration with our baby, it can be helpful to gain some empathy for them in the moment. One way to establish empathy is to put yourself in another person's shoes and to try to understand their view. In order to establish a little more empathy and patience with your baby, it might be helpful to put yourself in your baby's 'booties.' Oftentimes when we are frustrated, we tend to focus on how *we* are feeling. When our baby is crying or fussing, we focus on how *we're* upset, frustrated, or discouraged. However, sometimes it can reduce our own frustration by trying to understand how it might feel for *them*. When my daughter was born, this is one of the skills I used frequently during my own SOS Mommy Moments. In the heat of the moment, I would oftentimes try to understand my daughter's perspective. I imagined what it was like for her to try to adjust to this new world as an infant. I imagined her transitioning from the stability of the womb to the new and unpredictable world around her. I imagined her own frustration about not being able to communicate her wants and needs. Having some empathy for what my little one was going through, helped me stay patient during those SOS Mommy Moments.

Read an Encouragement Letter/ Affirmations/ Encouraging Quotes

A great tool that can help new moms navigate their SOS Mommy Moments, is reading positive letters, affirmations, or encouraging quotes. I would encourage all new moms to write themselves an Encouragement Letter. An Encouragement Letter is a letter that you write to yourself that you can read when you are feeling down, frustrated, overwhelmed, or discouraged. Or, ask another mother who has been there before to write you an Encouragement Letter. During an SOS Mommy Moment, you can take out your letter and read it when you need some positive encouragement, whenever you are feeling discouraged, overwhelmed, or upset. If you are struggling to write your letter, ask yourself these questions: What would I want to hear during those moments when I am struggling? What would I want my friends to say to me in this moment?

Having an Encouragement Letter handy can help stop the train of negative thinking we oftentimes tell ourselves in those SOS Mommy Moments. Similarly, positive affirmations or reading encouraging quotes can be another useful tool to use during these stressful moments. When I would have a hard day, I would write in a gratitude journal. I would focus on what I was grateful for that day or what went well for me that day. It's amazing how shifting your focus from negative thinking to being grateful can shift your mood. Our thoughts are related to our feelings and to our behaviors. When we are able to shift our thinking, our mood often shifts as well.

Distinguish Between Problems and Inconveniences

As new moms, one of the most important things that we can do is to know the difference between types of stressors. When we are in the middle of an SOS Mommy Moment, we oftentimes have difficulty in seeing the reality of the situation and we might magnify the situation. One of the best things that new moms can do, is to know the difference between a *problem* and an *inconvenience*. As author Robert Fulghum notes, it is important to "*know the difference between an inconvenience and a problem. If you break your neck, if you have nothing to eat, if your house is on fire, you got a problem. Everything else is just inconvenience. Life is inconvenient. Life is lumpy…A lump in the oatmeal – a lump in the throat – and a lump in the breast – are not the same lump. We should learn to know the difference.*" Many times I see new mothers blur the lines between these types of stressors. When they are in their SOS Mommy Moment, they view their inconvenience as a major problem. In these moments, it can be helpful to ask yourself, "Is this a problem? Or an inconvenience?" These simple questions can help distinguish between these types of stressors. For example, is it really a serious problem that my baby is irritable because she missed her nap? Or is this an inconvenience. Is it really a problem that my baby blew out his diaper and got it all over the car seat? Or an inconvenience? Knowing the difference between a problem and inconvenience can help new moms get a more realistic perspective of the situation as well as help them see the light at the end of the tunnel in their SOS Mommy Moment.

When All Else Fails...Ride the Wave

There is a useful tool in Dialectical Behavioral Therapy, created by Marsha Linehan, called riding the wave. Many days, we feel as though we are in the storm of parenthood, stranded in the middle of the ocean. We are on choppy waters, just trying to hold on and stay afloat. We try different approaches to try to help us stabilize and reach ashore, but our efforts don't seem to help much. When all of our approaches seem to be failing us, sometimes all we can do is ride the wave. When we ride the wave, we sit with our uncomfortable emotion until it passes and eventually reaches the shore. We recognize that our uncomfortable emotion will end eventually. Eventually, we will be on solid ground again. The storm will pass, because storms never last indefinitely. Some moments, all you can do is ride the wave of motherhood. Just knowing that you will survive this, because bad days or moments do not last forever, can help you get through the moment. Eventually the storm will clear and the sun will come out again. Whether you practice deep breathing, read your encouragement letter, or ride the wave, navigating SOS Mommy Moments are crucial to helping new moms stay emotionally resilient.

Chapter 10

Practice #9: Take Back Order

Organization is the foundation to get the rest of my life in gear.
– Kathy Lipp

Every mother is familiar with this scene: laundry baskets overflowing with clothes, toys thrown like confetti on the living room carpet, spilled milk on the kitchen floor. I could go on, but I'm feeling overwhelmed just thinking about it. When you are used to being organized, it can be a big wake up call to be thrown into this new parent life where it seems your environment is turned upside down. I'm one of those people who feels disorganized in the inside when my surroundings are scattered. When there is some semblance of neatness and organization in my life, I feel more relaxed, calm, and at ease. Turns out, I'm not alone. Research by NiCole Keith and colleagues found a link between individuals with clean houses and their health and activity level. Additional research has shown that an increase in visual stimuli (i.e., clutter) can affect our focus and efficiency of task completion (McMain & Kastner, 2011).

I hear this all the time with my therapy patients too. Not just the new moms, but all patients. I often hear that clutter and disorganization can increase their anxiety and stress levels.

Very often it happens that one of the first things that new mothers abandon, is order. But order helps us feel organized and gives us clarity. When we lose our order and organization, we can feel anxious, overwhelmed, and exhausted. Unfortunately, some research has shown that general cognitive functioning, executive functioning, and memory are poorer in pregnant women (Davies, et al., 2018). And after the baby is born, reduced sleep can also have an effect on cognition. Why is this important? Because executive functioning skills (i.e., planning, judgement, decision making, etc.) and memory are important in staying organized and with task completion. So not only do we see an increase in responsibility for new mothers but we may have more difficulty cognitively in accomplishing those responsibilities. Therefore, we need to find new skills and coping strategies to stay on top of things.

Simplify

One of the first things we can do when we find ourselves with increased responsibilities is to simplify, which will make things easier for us and reduce unnecessary and excess tasks or details. For example, before I had kids, I would go to the grocery store about five times per week and spend each night creating these elaborate meals. Mainly because I had the time to do this and I enjoy cooking. However, after I had kids, I had to simplify my process. I started making a grocery list and adding items to the list whenever I thought of them. Then on Fridays I would go to the grocery store and pick up the items I needed. I also discovered the beauty of online grocery ordering and pick-up. This simplified the process and gave me whole lot of time back. Instead of cooking elaborate meals most nights, I cook these meals maybe once or twice a week now. We still eat healthy, but we are just more organized about planning ahead. In his book *Simplify*, Joshua Becker discusses ways to find more simplicity in your life: through decreasing your time commitments, or decreasing your possessions. The example above is a way to decrease time commitments. One of the new mothers I worked with in therapy struggled with the second way. She had so many 'baby possessions' she felt that they were interfering in life. She discussed wanting all the new and shiny baby items and she registered for so many of them for her baby shower. While she was excited at first, she soon realized that not only were these possessions unnecessary but she didn't have room for them all. Were four baby swings really necessary? Also, she had so many baby clothes that she estimated that her son could make it longer than a month without her having to do laundry. However, his closet was a disaster because she didn't have room for everything. She started to realize that sometimes, less is more, in the possession department. She wanted to simplify, so she made a list of possessions she could reduce in her life. She ended up giving a lot of these baby possessions away to charity and a close friend who was pregnant. She discussed feeling 'lighter' after she simplified. As a new mother, it can be helpful to ask yourself: *What is unnecessarily time consuming in my life that can be shortened or simplified?* Or *what items in my life seem distracting or unimportant?* It can be helpful to get feedback or advice from other moms about this too.

Prioritize

Another helpful organization strategy is to prioritize. Since we only have so much time in our day, we need to figure out what are those tasks and responsibilities that are most important to complete and which tasks can be postponed or maybe even dropped all together. One strategy can be to create a To Do List with two sections: a 'soon' list and a 'later' list. The things you add to the 'soon' list are obviously higher on the priority scale than tasks on your 'later' list, and you can review your list regularly. Maybe after you review, some tasks on your later list continue to stay on the later list but sometimes they get moved up to the soon section. Or you can make one To Do list and number the top three items that are highest on the priority scale and accomplish those first. After those tasks are completed and crossed off, you can then number the next three highest priority tasks left on the list. You may find that some things that were previously high on the priority list, are now lower on the list. Our priorities and expectations change, and that's to be expected.

Delegate

Another strategy to help with organization and task completion is to delegate responsibilities to others when able. This is similar to the practice related to asking for help.

If we allow others to help us, it takes a lot of that stress and responsibility off of ourselves. If you have a partner, you could delegate tasks to them and split up your To Do list. At our house, my husband or I will put our initials by the tasks we will be responsible for completing. Now that my kids are out of the infancy stage, I can delegate small responsibilities to them (e.g., having them practice cleaning up their toys, helping to clean up spills with a paper towel, or dusting.) My 4-year-old loves to take the hand vacuum and pick up little food crumbs on the floor. Is the dusting job going to be as great as if I did it myself? Not likely. But that's OK with me. Getting every speck of dust out of my house is not high on the priority list for me. For new mom with infants, it will be a while before your kids can help. However, you can still delegate to others. In addition to a partner, many times friends or family members love to help out. Part of delegating is saying 'yes' to others' invitations to help. As mentioned before, I oftentimes hear, "But I don't want to burden others." Honestly, just like you feel good about helping others, other people like to help too. It makes them feel good. In fact, research provided by the Action for Happiness shows that doing things for others can have a positive impact on people's overall happiness and wellbeing. My dad is one of those people. He loves to be helpful. Whenever he comes to visit, he likes to do whatever he can to help out around the house. It makes him feel productive and it feels good for him to help. And, of course, I am so thankful for his help. Or maybe you've realized that it's worth getting a cleaning service once a month. That's delegation too. I have a close friend who began delegating her vacuuming to her new purchase 'Robbie' the Roomba vacuum. Robbie vacuums her whole house while she drinks her coffee. Whatever works. The point is, there are many ways to delegate.

Use Organization Tools

In addition to simplifying, prioritizing, and delegating, it can be beneficial to use organization tools. These tools might include lists (as discussed above), calendars, reminders on your phone, etc. Visual or auditory reminders can be extremely useful for staying organized. As mentioned before, potential difficulties with executive functioning and memory can sometimes affect our ability to organize, plan, and remember things in early parenthood. Thus, having these organization tools can be a good way to compensate for any potential challenges. I can't tell you how many new mothers say, "I think I have ADHD" (aka Attention Deficit/Hyperactivity Disorder). They say they get distracted easily, feel disorganized, struggle with staying focused, and struggle with task completion. However, ADHD is classified as a neurodevelopmental disorder that begins in childhood and not something you acquire from becoming a parent. But ADHD affects executive functioning, so I get why this can be frequently assumed. Using organization tools can help with planning, remembering tasks, and helping one feel more organized. In addition to organizational tools, other strategies that can be helpful include breaking up large projects down into smaller tasks, reducing external distractions when completing a task or project, keep frequently used items in a consistent place, and allow for breaks to help refresh attention. It can also be helpful to stick to a routine for completing tasks. Not only will it help you remember to complete the task but it will also help develop a habit so you can be more successful at taking back your order.

Reassess Your Finances

As many new mothers come to find out, having kids can be expensive. Adding another person to your family costs money. There are so many new necessities to buy that were likely not part of the picture before: diapers, formula, crib, toys, clothes, medical bills, etc. Due to the added expenses, it can be beneficial during pregnancy or early parenthood to reassess your finances. Part of staying financially organized as a new parent will likely include updating your budget and expenses. Those previous tools of prioritizing and simplifying things in your life will come in handy while updating your budget. For a lot of people, in order to have money to spend on these new items, they will need to reduce the amount of money spent in other areas of their life. Now is a good time to ask yourself, "What are some things I can reduce or eliminate in my life?" Going through a quick reassessment of your finances can help with staying organized and helping new parents with maintaining a sense of order in the home.

Afterword: Moving Forward and Getting Through Roadblocks

Determination gives you the resolve to keep going,
in spite of the roadblocks that lay before you.
– Denis Waitley

The previous ten chapters of this book explored many practices new moms can utilize to help them successfully navigate through the journey of early motherhood. But this book may not be helpful unless the discussed practices are actually implemented. In other words, while it can be important to *learn* these practices and specific skills, it's just as important to *apply* them. What good are the skills if you struggle with applying them, right? Which brings us to this point in the book. This chapter focuses on creating a plan to move forward and discusses ways to get through roadblocks or obstacles. Common roadblocks that may get in the way of progress are explored, as well as ways to move through the obstacles.

Common Obstacles

I would say the most common obstacle I hear from new moms that might prevent them from implementing the Practices is: *I don't have the time.* And I get this one. I really do. Early motherhood is busy and time consuming. We have a lot more responsibility than we did before our baby was born. However, sometimes if we don't put a little bit of time up front, then it costs us more time in the end. A common analogy might be this: let's pretend you are driving in your car and your check engine light goes on. You don't have time to take the car into the shop, but most likely you do it anyway. Why? Because you recognize that if you don't take care of it, it may become a bigger problem that will take up *more* time later on and will be *more* stressful than it would have if you just took care of the problem from the beginning. An easy solution might involve the practice of Taking Back Order. If we spend a little time each day simplifying, prioritizing, and delegating, then we may prevent the buildup of a larger physical and emotional problem later on. Spending a little time each day might actually save you time in the long run.

Another common obstacle that can sometimes get in the way of utilizing these practices is: *I forgot.* And this one I also understand, probably because I hear myself saying this a lot. I mean, I have every intention of utilizing a practice, but with all of the other things going on in a day, it's just too easy to forget. So, how do you set yourself up for success? For me, the easiest thing to do is to write down my practice goals. You can identify one or two practices that you realize might be weak areas for you. After you identify those, write down small goals related to the practices you chose. For example, for me I realized that taking back order and securing help and support from others were weak areas for me. Writing down your goals can help you be more successful with your goal. It can help transform it from a conceptual thought to a plan. Also, having a piece of paper around a common area of your house with your goals written down can help remind you of your plan and bring back focus to your goals. Another tool that can help you remember your goal is to schedule it into a calendar or somehow make it part of your daily routine. For example, with self-care, you might schedule self-care strategies onto your calendar. Or you might make it part of your daily routine by practicing it at the same time every day. One of my co-workers would keep a journal next to her bed and journal for five minutes every night before bed. She said this helped with self-care by reducing her stress before bed. I had another friend who decided that every morning she would read a short, inspirational quote to set off her day on a positive note. These are things that might take minutes out of your day. And by doing them consistently and repetitively every day, they become a habit into your routine. This in turn can help you remember and be more successful with your goal.

Another common obstacle new moms often note is: *It's too much effort.* I hear it all the time. Again, it makes sense. Sometimes we are just too tired to do one more thing. And usually when our battery is drained, we feel even more tired. When we have been giving all day, and we have nothing left to give, we feel exhausted. Unfortunately, this might indicate that we need to focus on our practices even more. It's helpful to start small. Instead of setting a goal to go to the gym, you could start by running the stairs or doing a shorter exercise video at home. Set yourself up for success instead of failure. You are more likely to be successful if you start with small steps. Having a goal that is too big can be overwhelming. Oftentimes when we feel overwhelmed, we give up our goal, procrastinate, or feel like we have failed. Obviously, this is not helpful. So, start with small goals.

Another frequent roadblock I hear is: *I feel guilty about spending time or focusing on myself.* As new moms, it is a common misconception that we are supposed to neglect ourselves in order to put our full time, focus, and attention onto our child. But as we discussed before, this can be problematic in the long run. I'm sure many of you have heard the 'oxygen mask' metaphor, and it does truly fit in this scenario. This relates to being on an airplane when the flight crew reminds you to put on your own oxygen mask before assisting others in the case of an emergency. This metaphor can be prevalent in parenting at times too. In order for us to be the best mothers to our children, we also need to take care of ourselves. It's not a consideration, but rather a necessity. Overall, when it comes to common obstacles or roadblocks, it can be important to shift your focus from *I can't because…*to *How can I?*

Conclusion

While it will be one of the most wonderful things a woman will do in her lifetime, becoming a mother can also be one of the biggest transitions she will face. The purpose of this book is to give new mothers tips and strategies to help stay emotionally strong and healthy during this transition. We discussed the importance of reevaluating expectations and beliefs about motherhood. We discussed the importance of establishing a bond with your baby and asking for help when needed. We explored the benefits of changing negative self-talk and how to incorporate self-care strategies into our lives. We focused on making sure to incorporate all roles of your personal identity and to evolve the relationship with your partner. We also discussed the importance of navigating through those difficult SOS Mommy Moments and the benefits of taking back order in our lives. Yes, having children can lead to some big changes and can even be challenging at times. But yet, so many people decide to become parents in their lifetime. Many people would argue that this is because the rewards of parenthood outnumber and outweigh the difficulties you may experience. There is no comparable feeling to hearing your child say "I love you" for the first time. With kids, you get to see the world though fresh eyes. You begin to notice more and think about things in a way you maybe haven't for a very long time. You appreciate the little things in life that you might have previously had taken for granted. You begin to have a deeper understanding of your partner. You get to grow as a person by becoming more patient, understanding, and empathetic. You get to be a VIP to this little person and become the most important thing in their world. You get to find another, added purpose to your life that can help give you a whole new outlook and meaning on life itself. And lastly, you get to find out how strong and amazing you truly are. So, congratulations! I hope you fully enjoy and experience the wonder that this new journey of motherhood brings.

References

Badr, H.A., and Zauszniewski, J.A. (2017). Kangaroo care and postpartum depression: The role of oxytocin. *International Journal of Nursing Sciences*, 4(2): 179–183.

Benson, H., and Klipper, M.Z. (1992). The Relaxation Response. Harper Collins, New York.

Buck, R. (1980). Nonverbal behavior and the theory of emotion: The facial feedback hypothesis. *Journal of Personality and Social Psychology, 38*(5), 811–824.

Campbell-Yeo M, Disher T, Benoit B, Johnston C. (2015). Understanding kangaroo care and its benefits to preterm infants. *Pediatric Health, Medicine, and Therapeutics,* 6: 15–32

Corrigan, C.P., Kwasky, A.N., and Groh, C.J. (2015). Social Support, postpartum depression, and professional assistance: A survey of mothers in the Midwestern United States. *The Journal of Perinatal Education,* 24(1).

Davies, S.J, Ag Lum, J., Skouteris, H., Byrne, L.K., Hayden, M.J. (2018). Cognitive impairment during pregnancy: A meta-analysis. *The Medical Journal of Australia*, 208(1): 35–40.

Fulghum, R., Caldwell, D. (1999). All I Really Need to Know I Learned in Kindergarten. United States: Dramatic Pub.

Gottman, J.M., & Gottman, J.S. (2007). And Baby Makes Three. New York: Crown.

Holmes, T.H. & Rahe, R.H. (1967). The Social Readjustment Rating Scale. *Journal of Psychosomatic Research,* 11: 213–218.

Kross, E., Bruehlman-Senecal, E., Park, J., Burson, A., Dougherty, A., Shablack, H., Bremner, R., Moser, J., and Ayduk, O. (2014). Self-talk as a regulatory mechanism: How you do it matters. *Journal of Personality and Social Psychology*, 106(2): 304–324

Levine, A., Zagoory-Sharon, O., Feldman, R., Weller, A. (2007). Oxytocin during pregnancy and early postpartum: Individual patterns and maternal-fetal attachment. *Peptides*, 28(6): 1162–1169.

Linehan, M.M. (2014). DBT Skills Training Manual, Second Edition. New York: Guildford Publications.

Maslow, A.H. (1970). Motivation and Personality. (Rev. Ed.). New York: Harper and Row.

McMains, S. and Kastner, S. (2011). Interactions of top-down and bottom-up mechanisms in human visual cortex. *The Journal of Neuroscience*, 12 (31): 587–597.

Nilsson, U. (2009). Soothing music can increase oxytocin levels during bed rest after open-heart surgery: a randomized control trial. *Journal of Clinical Nursing*, 18(15): 2153–2161.

Poobalan AS, Aucott LS, Ross L, Smith WC, Helms PJ, Williams JH. (2007). Effects of treating postnatal depression on mother-infant interaction and child development: systematic review. *The British Journal of Psychiatry,* Nov; 191: 378–386.

Small, M.F. (1998). How Biology and Culture Shape the Way We Parent. New York: Anchor Books.

Brown, B. (2015) Rising Strong. Random House, New York.

Websites:

https://newsinfo.iu.edu/web/page/normal/14627.html

Pregnancy and Postpartum Support
https://ppsupportmn.org/what-are-pmads/